Dream journal

Keep Track Books

Keep Track Books brings you a variety of
essential notebooks and journals — including
dream journals with the same interior as this one,
but with different cover designs.

Please visit www.lusciousbooks.co.uk to find out more.

CreateSpace, Charleston SC
Design © Keep Track Books

Dreams are precious gifts

They are windows to your innermost self and through them you can learn more about
your subconscious feelings, increase your self-awareness, access your creativity
and be guided by your inner wisdom.

How to use this dream journal

Dreams are easily lost if they are not written down. Therefore, it's good to keep
your dream journal by your bed and write down your dream as soon as you wake up.
If you can't remember the whole dream, write down any feelings, thoughts or
images that come to mind. Don't judge what you're writing – just let everything
flow onto the page freely. Once you have done this, give your dream a title
and add the date.

This journal contains prompts to help you analyse and interpret your dreams.
You don't have to fill in all the sections and you don't have to answer the questions
in the order that they are laid out on the page. Start by filling in the sections
that feel the easiest to answer.

You don't have to write down your dream and interpret it all in one go.
If you feel that the answers are not flowing easily, leave the analysis for another time.
Sometimes it takes a while to fully understand what a specific dream is about.

May your dream exploration be filled with
exciting discoveries and profound insights!

Dream title: _____   Date: _____

Dream description

....
....
....
....
....
....
....
....
....
....
....
....
....
....
....
....
....
....
....
....
....
....
....
....
....
....
....
....

Was this dream...

	a recurring dream?	a lucid dream?	a nightmare?
	☐ Yes ☐ No	☐ Yes ☐ No	☐ Yes ☐ No

What were the key themes or issues in the dream?

....

....

....

What were your prominent emotions and feelings?

☐ Happiness	☐ Surprise	☐ Indifference	☐ Fear	☐ Disapproval
☐ Love	☐ Joy	☐ Sadness	☐ Panic	☐ Rejection
☐ Freedom	☐ Contentment	☐ Frustration	☐ Envy	☐ Anxiety
☐ Compassion	☐ Pride	☐ Betrayal	☐ Jealousy	☐ Guilt
☐ Arousal	☐ Confusion	☐ Anger	☐ Shame	☐ Pain

Other?

☐ .... ☐ ....

☐ .... ☐ ....

Could this dream relate to a recent situation/event/person/problem in your life?

....

....

....

What is your interpretation of the dream?

....

....

....

....

....

....

....

In what way(s) does this dream affect you?
Does it provide clarity into something or suggest a specific course of action?

....

....

....

Dream title: _____ Date:

Dream description

....
....
....
....
....
....
....
....
....
....
....
....
....
....
....
....
....
....
....
....
....
....
....
....
....
....
....
....
....
....
....

Was this dream...   a recurring dream?   a lucid dream?   a nightmare?
                         ☐ Yes ☐ No   ☐ Yes ☐ No   ☐ Yes ☐ No

What were the key themes or issues in the dream?

....

....

....

What were your prominent emotions and feelings?

☐ Happiness	☐ Surprise	☐ Indifference	☐ Fear	☐ Disapproval
☐ Love	☐ Joy	☐ Sadness	☐ Panic	☐ Rejection
☐ Freedom	☐ Contentment	☐ Frustration	☐ Envy	☐ Anxiety
☐ Compassion	☐ Pride	☐ Betrayal	☐ Jealousy	☐ Guilt
☐ Arousal	☐ Confusion	☐ Anger	☐ Shame	☐ Pain

Other?   ☐ ....   ☐ ....

           ☐ ....   ☐ ....

Could this dream relate to a recent situation/event/person/problem in your life?

....

....

....

What is your interpretation of the dream?

....

....

....

....

....

....

....

In what way(s) does this dream affect you?
Does it provide clarity into something or suggest a specific course of action?

....

....

....

Dream title: _____   Date: _____

Dream description

....
....
....
....
....
....
....
....
....
....
....
....
....
....
....
....
....
....
....
....
....
....
....
....
....
....
....
....

Was this dream...   a recurring dream?   a lucid dream?   a nightmare?
                             ☐ Yes ☐ No   ☐ Yes ☐ No   ☐ Yes ☐ No

What were the key themes or issues in the dream?

....

....

....

What were your prominent emotions and feelings?

☐ Happiness	☐ Surprise	☐ Indifference	☐ Fear	☐ Disapproval
☐ Love	☐ Joy	☐ Sadness	☐ Panic	☐ Rejection
☐ Freedom	☐ Contentment	☐ Frustration	☐ Envy	☐ Anxiety
☐ Compassion	☐ Pride	☐ Betrayal	☐ Jealousy	☐ Guilt
☐ Arousal	☐ Confusion	☐ Anger	☐ Shame	☐ Pain
Other?	☐		☐	
	☐		☐	

Could this dream relate to a recent situation/event/person/problem in your life?

....

....

....

What is your interpretation of the dream?

....

....

....

....

....

....

....

In what way(s) does this dream affect you?
Does it provide clarity into something or suggest a specific course of action?

....

....

....

Dream title: _____   Date: _____

Dream description

....
....
....
....
....
....
....
....
....
....
....
....
....
....
....
....
....
....
....
....
....
....
....
....
....
....
....
....

Was this dream...   a recurring dream?   a lucid dream?   a nightmare?
                           ☐ Yes ☐ No   ☐ Yes ☐ No   ☐ Yes ☐ No

What were the key themes or issues in the dream?

....

....

....

What were your prominent emotions and feelings?

☐ Happiness	☐ Surprise	☐ Indifference	☐ Fear	☐ Disapproval
☐ Love	☐ Joy	☐ Sadness	☐ Panic	☐ Rejection
☐ Freedom	☐ Contentment	☐ Frustration	☐ Envy	☐ Anxiety
☐ Compassion	☐ Pride	☐ Betrayal	☐ Jealousy	☐ Guilt
☐ Arousal	☐ Confusion	☐ Anger	☐ Shame	☐ Pain

Other?   ☐ ....   ☐ ....

           ☐ ....   ☐ ....

Could this dream relate to a recent situation/event/person/problem in your life?

....

....

....

What is your interpretation of the dream?

....

....

....

....

....

....

....

In what way(s) does this dream affect you?
Does it provide clarity into something or suggest a specific course of action?

....

....

....

Dream title: Date:

Dream description

....
....
....
....
....
....
....
....
....
....
....
....
....
....
....
....
....
....
....
....
....
....
....
....
....
....
....
....
....
....
....
....
....

Was this dream...   a recurring dream?   a lucid dream?   a nightmare?
                      ☐ Yes ☐ No   ☐ Yes ☐ No   ☐ Yes ☐ No

What were the key themes or issues in the dream?

....
....
....

What were your prominent emotions and feelings?

☐ Happiness   ☐ Surprise   ☐ Indifference   ☐ Fear   ☐ Disapproval
☐ Love   ☐ Joy   ☐ Sadness   ☐ Panic   ☐ Rejection
☐ Freedom   ☐ Contentment   ☐ Frustration   ☐ Envy   ☐ Anxiety
☐ Compassion   ☐ Pride   ☐ Betrayal   ☐ Jealousy   ☐ Guilt
☐ Arousal   ☐ Confusion   ☐ Anger   ☐ Shame   ☐ Pain
Other?   ☐ ....   ☐ ....
                 ☐ ....   ☐ ....

Could this dream relate to a recent situation/event/person/problem in your life?

....
....
....

What is your interpretation of the dream?

....
....
....
....
....
....
....

In what way(s) does this dream affect you?
Does it provide clarity into something or suggest a specific course of action?

....
....
....

Dream title: _____ Date: _____

Dream description

....
....
....
....
....
....
....
....
....
....
....
....
....
....
....
....
....
....
....
....
....
....
....
....
....
....
....
....
....
....
....

Was this dream...   a recurring dream?   a lucid dream?   a nightmare?
☐ Yes ☐ No   ☐ Yes ☐ No   ☐ Yes ☐ No

What were the key themes or issues in the dream?

....

....

....

What were your prominent emotions and feelings?

☐ Happiness	☐ Surprise	☐ Indifference	☐ Fear	☐ Disapproval
☐ Love	☐ Joy	☐ Sadness	☐ Panic	☐ Rejection
☐ Freedom	☐ Contentment	☐ Frustration	☐ Envy	☐ Anxiety
☐ Compassion	☐ Pride	☐ Betrayal	☐ Jealousy	☐ Guilt
☐ Arousal	☐ Confusion	☐ Anger	☐ Shame	☐ Pain

Other?   ☐ ....   ☐ ....

☐ ....   ☐ ....

Could this dream relate to a recent situation/event/person/problem in your life?

....

....

....

What is your interpretation of the dream?

....

....

....

....

....

....

....

In what way(s) does this dream affect you?
Does it provide clarity into something or suggest a specific course of action?

....

....

....

Dream title: _____   Date: _____

Dream description
....
....
....
....
....
....
....
....
....
....
....
....
....
....
....
....
....
....
....
....
....
....
....
....
....
....
....
....
....

Was this dream...   a recurring dream?   a lucid dream?   a nightmare?
☐ Yes ☐ No   ☐ Yes ☐ No   ☐ Yes ☐ No

What were the key themes or issues in the dream?

....
....
....

What were your prominent emotions and feelings?

☐ Happiness	☐ Surprise	☐ Indifference	☐ Fear	☐ Disapproval
☐ Love	☐ Joy	☐ Sadness	☐ Panic	☐ Rejection
☐ Freedom	☐ Contentment	☐ Frustration	☐ Envy	☐ Anxiety
☐ Compassion	☐ Pride	☐ Betrayal	☐ Jealousy	☐ Guilt
☐ Arousal	☐ Confusion	☐ Anger	☐ Shame	☐ Pain

Other?
☐ ....   ☐ ....
☐ ....   ☐ ....

Could this dream relate to a recent situation/event/person/problem in your life?

....
....
....

What is your interpretation of the dream?

....
....
....
....
....
....
....

In what way(s) does this dream affect you?
Does it provide clarity into something or suggest a specific course of action?

....
....
....

Dream title: _____ Date: _____

Dream description

....

....

....

....

....

....

....

....

....

....

....

....

....

....

....

....

....

....

....

....

....

....

....

....

....

....

....

....

....

....

Was this dream...   a recurring dream?   a lucid dream?   a nightmare?
☐ Yes ☐ No   ☐ Yes ☐ No   ☐ Yes ☐ No

What were the key themes or issues in the dream?

....

....

....

What were your prominent emotions and feelings?

☐ Happiness	☐ Surprise	☐ Indifference	☐ Fear	☐ Disapproval
☐ Love	☐ Joy	☐ Sadness	☐ Panic	☐ Rejection
☐ Freedom	☐ Contentment	☐ Frustration	☐ Envy	☐ Anxiety
☐ Compassion	☐ Pride	☐ Betrayal	☐ Jealousy	☐ Guilt
☐ Arousal	☐ Confusion	☐ Anger	☐ Shame	☐ Pain

Other?   ☐ ....   ☐ ....

☐ ....   ☐ ....

Could this dream relate to a recent situation/event/person/problem in your life?

....

....

....

What is your interpretation of the dream?

....

....

....

....

....

....

....

In what way(s) does this dream affect you?
Does it provide clarity into something or suggest a specific course of action?

....

....

....

Dream title: _____ Date: _____

Dream description

....
....
....
....
....
....
....
....
....
....
....
....
....
....
....
....
....
....
....
....
....
....
....
....
....
....
....
....
....
....
....

Was this dream...   a recurring dream?   a lucid dream?   a nightmare?
☐ Yes ☐ No   ☐ Yes ☐ No   ☐ Yes ☐ No

What were the key themes or issues in the dream?

....
....
....

What were your prominent emotions and feelings?

☐ Happiness	☐ Surprise	☐ Indifference	☐ Fear	☐ Disapproval
☐ Love	☐ Joy	☐ Sadness	☐ Panic	☐ Rejection
☐ Freedom	☐ Contentment	☐ Frustration	☐ Envy	☐ Anxiety
☐ Compassion	☐ Pride	☐ Betrayal	☐ Jealousy	☐ Guilt
☐ Arousal	☐ Confusion	☐ Anger	☐ Shame	☐ Pain

Other?   ☐ ....   ☐ ....

☐ ....   ☐ ....

Could this dream relate to a recent situation/event/person/problem in your life?

....
....
....

What is your interpretation of the dream?

....
....
....
....
....
....

In what way(s) does this dream affect you?
Does it provide clarity into something or suggest a specific course of action?

....
....
....

Dream title: _____ Date: _____

Dream description

....
....
....
....
....
....
....
....
....
....
....
....
....
....
....
....
....
....
....
....
....
....
....
....
....
....
....
....
....
....

Was this dream... a recurring dream? a lucid dream? a nightmare?

☐ Yes ☐ No ☐ Yes ☐ No ☐ Yes ☐ No

What were the key themes or issues in the dream?

....
....
....

What were your prominent emotions and feelings?

☐ Happiness	☐ Surprise	☐ Indifference	☐ Fear	☐ Disapproval
☐ Love	☐ Joy	☐ Sadness	☐ Panic	☐ Rejection
☐ Freedom	☐ Contentment	☐ Frustration	☐ Envy	☐ Anxiety
☐ Compassion	☐ Pride	☐ Betrayal	☐ Jealousy	☐ Guilt
☐ Arousal	☐ Confusion	☐ Anger	☐ Shame	☐ Pain

Other?
☐ .... ☐ ....
☐ .... ☐ ....

Could this dream relate to a recent situation/event/person/problem in your life?

....
....
....

What is your interpretation of the dream?

....
....
....
....
....
....
....

In what way(s) does this dream affect you?
Does it provide clarity into something or suggest a specific course of action?

....
....
....

Dream title: _____ Date: _____

Dream description

....
....
....
....
....
....
....
....
....
....
....
....
....
....
....
....
....
....
....
....
....
....
....
....
....
....

Was this dream...   a recurring dream?   a lucid dream?   a nightmare?
                        ☐ Yes ☐ No   ☐ Yes ☐ No   ☐ Yes ☐ No

What were the key themes or issues in the dream?

....

....

....

What were your prominent emotions and feelings?

☐ Happiness	☐ Surprise	☐ Indifference	☐ Fear	☐ Disapproval
☐ Love	☐ Joy	☐ Sadness	☐ Panic	☐ Rejection
☐ Freedom	☐ Contentment	☐ Frustration	☐ Envy	☐ Anxiety
☐ Compassion	☐ Pride	☐ Betrayal	☐ Jealousy	☐ Guilt
☐ Arousal	☐ Confusion	☐ Anger	☐ Shame	☐ Pain

Other?   ☐ ....   ☐ ....

           ☐ ....   ☐ ....

Could this dream relate to a recent situation/event/person/problem in your life?

....

....

....

What is your interpretation of the dream?

....

....

....

....

....

....

....

In what way(s) does this dream affect you?
Does it provide clarity into something or suggest a specific course of action?

....

....

....

Dream title: _____   Date: _____

Dream description

....
....
....
....
....
....
....
....
....
....
....
....
....
....
....
....
....
....
....
....
....
....
....
....
....
....
....
....
....
....
....
....

Was this dream...   a recurring dream?   a lucid dream?   a nightmare?
                     ☐ Yes ☐ No   ☐ Yes ☐ No   ☐ Yes ☐ No

What were the key themes or issues in the dream?

....
....
....

What were your prominent emotions and feelings?

☐ Happiness	☐ Surprise	☐ Indifference	☐ Fear	☐ Disapproval
☐ Love	☐ Joy	☐ Sadness	☐ Panic	☐ Rejection
☐ Freedom	☐ Contentment	☐ Frustration	☐ Envy	☐ Anxiety
☐ Compassion	☐ Pride	☐ Betrayal	☐ Jealousy	☐ Guilt
☐ Arousal	☐ Confusion	☐ Anger	☐ Shame	☐ Pain
Other?	☐		☐	
	☐		☐	

Could this dream relate to a recent situation/event/person/problem in your life?

....
....
....

What is your interpretation of the dream?

....
....
....
....
....
....
....

In what way(s) does this dream affect you?
Does it provide clarity into something or suggest a specific course of action?

....
....
....

Dream title: Date:

Dream description

....
....
....
....
....
....
....
....
....
....
....
....
....
....
....
....
....
....
....
....
....
....
....
....
....
....
....
....
....
....
....

Was this dream... a recurring dream? a lucid dream? a nightmare?

☐ Yes ☐ No ☐ Yes ☐ No ☐ Yes ☐ No

What were the key themes or issues in the dream?

....

....

....

What were your prominent emotions and feelings?

☐ Happiness	☐ Surprise	☐ Indifference	☐ Fear	☐ Disapproval
☐ Love	☐ Joy	☐ Sadness	☐ Panic	☐ Rejection
☐ Freedom	☐ Contentment	☐ Frustration	☐ Envy	☐ Anxiety
☐ Compassion	☐ Pride	☐ Betrayal	☐ Jealousy	☐ Guilt
☐ Arousal	☐ Confusion	☐ Anger	☐ Shame	☐ Pain

Other? ☐ .... ☐ ....

☐ .... ☐ ....

Could this dream relate to a recent situation/event/person/problem in your life?

....

....

....

What is your interpretation of the dream?

....

....

....

....

....

....

....

In what way(s) does this dream affect you?
Does it provide clarity into something or suggest a specific course of action?

....

....

....

Dream title: Date:

Dream description

Was this dream...　　a recurring dream?　　a lucid dream?　　a nightmare?
　　　　　　　　　　☐ Yes ☐ No　　☐ Yes ☐ No　　☐ Yes ☐ No

What were the key themes or issues in the dream?

....
....
....

What were your prominent emotions and feelings?

☐ Happiness	☐ Surprise	☐ Indifference	☐ Fear	☐ Disapproval
☐ Love	☐ Joy	☐ Sadness	☐ Panic	☐ Rejection
☐ Freedom	☐ Contentment	☐ Frustration	☐ Envy	☐ Anxiety
☐ Compassion	☐ Pride	☐ Betrayal	☐ Jealousy	☐ Guilt
☐ Arousal	☐ Confusion	☐ Anger	☐ Shame	☐ Pain
Other?	☐		☐	
	☐		☐	

Could this dream relate to a recent situation/event/person/problem in your life?

....
....
....

What is your interpretation of the dream?

....
....
....
....
....
....
....

In what way(s) does this dream affect you?
Does it provide clarity into something or suggest a specific course of action?

....
....
....

Dream title: _____ Date: _____

Dream description

....
....
....
....
....
....
....
....
....
....
....
....
....
....
....
....
....
....
....
....
....
....
....
....
....
....
....
....
....

Was this dream...

	a recurring dream?	a lucid dream?	a nightmare?
	☐ Yes ☐ No	☐ Yes ☐ No	☐ Yes ☐ No

What were the key themes or issues in the dream?

....

....

....

What were your prominent emotions and feelings?

☐ Happiness	☐ Surprise	☐ Indifference	☐ Fear	☐ Disapproval
☐ Love	☐ Joy	☐ Sadness	☐ Panic	☐ Rejection
☐ Freedom	☐ Contentment	☐ Frustration	☐ Envy	☐ Anxiety
☐ Compassion	☐ Pride	☐ Betrayal	☐ Jealousy	☐ Guilt
☐ Arousal	☐ Confusion	☐ Anger	☐ Shame	☐ Pain

Other?   ☐ ....   ☐ ....

☐ ....   ☐ ....

Could this dream relate to a recent situation/event/person/problem in your life?

....

....

....

What is your interpretation of the dream?

....

....

....

....

....

....

....

In what way(s) does this dream affect you?
Does it provide clarity into something or suggest a specific course of action?

....

....

....

Dream title: Date:

Dream description

....

....

....

....

....

....

....

....

....

....

....

....

....

....

....

....

....

....

....

....

....

....

....

....

....

....

....

....

....

....

Was this dream...   a recurring dream?   a lucid dream?   a nightmare?
                      ☐ Yes ☐ No   ☐ Yes ☐ No   ☐ Yes ☐ No

What were the key themes or issues in the dream?

....

....

....

What were your prominent emotions and feelings?

☐ Happiness	☐ Surprise	☐ Indifference	☐ Fear	☐ Disapproval
☐ Love	☐ Joy	☐ Sadness	☐ Panic	☐ Rejection
☐ Freedom	☐ Contentment	☐ Frustration	☐ Envy	☐ Anxiety
☐ Compassion	☐ Pride	☐ Betrayal	☐ Jealousy	☐ Guilt
☐ Arousal	☐ Confusion	☐ Anger	☐ Shame	☐ Pain

Other?   ☐ ....   ☐ ....

           ☐ ....   ☐ ....

Could this dream relate to a recent situation/event/person/problem in your life?

....

....

....

What is your interpretation of the dream?

....

....

....

....

....

....

....

In what way(s) does this dream affect you?
Does it provide clarity into something or suggest a specific course of action?

....

....

....

Dream title: Date:

Dream description

....

....

....

....

....

....

....

....

....

....

....

....

....

....

....

....

....

....

....

....

....

....

....

....

....

....

....

....

....

....

Was this dream...   a recurring dream?   a lucid dream?   a nightmare?
　　　　　　　　　　☐ Yes ☐ No   ☐ Yes ☐ No   ☐ Yes ☐ No

What were the key themes or issues in the dream?

....

....

....

What were your prominent emotions and feelings?

☐ Happiness	☐ Surprise	☐ Indifference	☐ Fear	☐ Disapproval
☐ Love	☐ Joy	☐ Sadness	☐ Panic	☐ Rejection
☐ Freedom	☐ Contentment	☐ Frustration	☐ Envy	☐ Anxiety
☐ Compassion	☐ Pride	☐ Betrayal	☐ Jealousy	☐ Guilt
☐ Arousal	☐ Confusion	☐ Anger	☐ Shame	☐ Pain

Other?   ☐ ....   ☐ ....
　　　　 ☐ ....   ☐ ....

Could this dream relate to a recent situation/event/person/problem in your life?

....

....

....

What is your interpretation of the dream?

....

....

....

....

....

....

....

In what way(s) does this dream affect you?
Does it provide clarity into something or suggest a specific course of action?

....

....

....

Dream title: Date:

Dream description

....
....
....
....
....
....
....
....
....
....
....
....
....
....
....
....
....
....
....
....
....
....
....
....
....
....
....
....
....
....
....

Was this dream...   a recurring dream?   a lucid dream?   a nightmare?

□ Yes □ No   □ Yes □ No   □ Yes □ No

What were the key themes or issues in the dream?

....

....

....

What were your prominent emotions and feelings?

□ Happiness	□ Surprise	□ Indifference	□ Fear	□ Disapproval
□ Love	□ Joy	□ Sadness	□ Panic	□ Rejection
□ Freedom	□ Contentment	□ Frustration	□ Envy	□ Anxiety
□ Compassion	□ Pride	□ Betrayal	□ Jealousy	□ Guilt
□ Arousal	□ Confusion	□ Anger	□ Shame	□ Pain

Other? □ .... □ ....

       □ .... □ ....

Could this dream relate to a recent situation/event/person/problem in your life?

....

....

....

What is your interpretation of the dream?

....

....

....

....

....

....

....

....

In what way(s) does this dream affect you?
Does it provide clarity into something or suggest a specific course of action?

....

....

....

Dream title: _____   Date: _____

Dream description

....
....
....
....
....
....
....
....
....
....
....
....
....
....
....
....
....
....
....
....
....
....
....
....
....
....
....
....
....
....

Was this dream...   a recurring dream?   a lucid dream?   a nightmare?
                     ☐ Yes   ☐ No   ☐ Yes   ☐ No   ☐ Yes   ☐ No

What were the key themes or issues in the dream?

....
....
....

What were your prominent emotions and feelings?

☐ Happiness   ☐ Surprise   ☐ Indifference   ☐ Fear   ☐ Disapproval
☐ Love   ☐ Joy   ☐ Sadness   ☐ Panic   ☐ Rejection
☐ Freedom   ☐ Contentment   ☐ Frustration   ☐ Envy   ☐ Anxiety
☐ Compassion   ☐ Pride   ☐ Betrayal   ☐ Jealousy   ☐ Guilt
☐ Arousal   ☐ Confusion   ☐ Anger   ☐ Shame   ☐ Pain
Other?   ☐   ☐ ....
                ☐ ....   ☐ ....

Could this dream relate to a recent situation/event/person/problem in your life?

....
....
....

What is your interpretation of the dream?

....
....
....
....
....
....
....

In what way(s) does this dream affect you?
Does it provide clarity into something or suggest a specific course of action?

....
....
....

Dream title: _____   Date: _____

Dream description

....
....
....
....
....
....
....
....
....
....
....
....
....
....
....
....
....
....
....
....
....
....
....
....
....
....
....
....
....
....
....
....

Was this dream... a recurring dream? a lucid dream? a nightmare?
☐ Yes ☐ No   ☐ Yes ☐ No   ☐ Yes ☐ No

What were the key themes or issues in the dream?

....

....

....

What were your prominent emotions and feelings?

☐ Happiness	☐ Surprise	☐ Indifference	☐ Fear	☐ Disapproval
☐ Love	☐ Joy	☐ Sadness	☐ Panic	☐ Rejection
☐ Freedom	☐ Contentment	☐ Frustration	☐ Envy	☐ Anxiety
☐ Compassion	☐ Pride	☐ Betrayal	☐ Jealousy	☐ Guilt
☐ Arousal	☐ Confusion	☐ Anger	☐ Shame	☐ Pain

Other?   ☐ ....   ☐ ....

☐ ....   ☐ ....

Could this dream relate to a recent situation/event/person/problem in your life?

....

....

....

What is your interpretation of the dream?

....

....

....

....

....

....

....

In what way(s) does this dream affect you?
Does it provide clarity into something or suggest a specific course of action?

....

....

....

Dream title: _____   Date: _____

Dream description

....
....
....
....
....
....
....
....
....
....
....
....
....
....
....
....
....
....
....
....
....
....
....
....
....
....
....
....
....
....
....
....

Was this dream...   a recurring dream?   a lucid dream?   a nightmare?
                     ☐ Yes ☐ No   ☐ Yes ☐ No   ☐ Yes ☐ No

What were the key themes or issues in the dream?

....

....

....

What were your prominent emotions and feelings?

☐ Happiness	☐ Surprise	☐ Indifference	☐ Fear	☐ Disapproval
☐ Love	☐ Joy	☐ Sadness	☐ Panic	☐ Rejection
☐ Freedom	☐ Contentment	☐ Frustration	☐ Envy	☐ Anxiety
☐ Compassion	☐ Pride	☐ Betrayal	☐ Jealousy	☐ Guilt
☐ Arousal	☐ Confusion	☐ Anger	☐ Shame	☐ Pain

Other?   ☐ ....   ☐ ....

☐ ....   ☐ ....

Could this dream relate to a recent situation/event/person/problem in your life?

....

....

....

What is your interpretation of the dream?

....

....

....

....

....

....

....

In what way(s) does this dream affect you?
Does it provide clarity into something or suggest a specific course of action?

....

....

....

Dream title: Date:

Dream description

Was this dream...   a recurring dream?   a lucid dream?   a nightmare?

☐ Yes ☐ No   ☐ Yes ☐ No   ☐ Yes ☐ No

What were the key themes or issues in the dream?

....

....

....

What were your prominent emotions and feelings?

☐ Happiness	☐ Surprise	☐ Indifference	☐ Fear	☐ Disapproval
☐ Love	☐ Joy	☐ Sadness	☐ Panic	☐ Rejection
☐ Freedom	☐ Contentment	☐ Frustration	☐ Envy	☐ Anxiety
☐ Compassion	☐ Pride	☐ Betrayal	☐ Jealousy	☐ Guilt
☐ Arousal	☐ Confusion	☐ Anger	☐ Shame	☐ Pain
Other?	☐		☐	
	☐		☐	

Could this dream relate to a recent situation/event/person/problem in your life?

....

....

....

What is your interpretation of the dream?

....

....

....

....

....

....

....

In what way(s) does this dream affect you?
Does it provide clarity into something or suggest a specific course of action?

....

....

....

Dream title: _____ Date: _____

Dream description

....

....

....

....

....

....

....

....

....

....

....

....

....

....

....

....

....

....

....

....

....

....

....

....

....

....

....

....

....

....

Was this dream...   a recurring dream?   a lucid dream?   a nightmare?
     ☐ Yes ☐ No   ☐ Yes ☐ No   ☐ Yes ☐ No

What were the key themes or issues in the dream?

....

....

....

What were your prominent emotions and feelings?

☐ Happiness	☐ Surprise	☐ Indifference	☐ Fear	☐ Disapproval
☐ Love	☐ Joy	☐ Sadness	☐ Panic	☐ Rejection
☐ Freedom	☐ Contentment	☐ Frustration	☐ Envy	☐ Anxiety
☐ Compassion	☐ Pride	☐ Betrayal	☐ Jealousy	☐ Guilt
☐ Arousal	☐ Confusion	☐ Anger	☐ Shame	☐ Pain
Other?	☐		☐	
	☐		☐	

Could this dream relate to a recent situation/event/person/problem in your life?

....

....

....

What is your interpretation of the dream?

....

....

....

....

....

....

....

In what way(s) does this dream affect you?
Does it provide clarity into something or suggest a specific course of action?

....

....

....

Dream title: Date:

Dream description

....
....
....
....
....
....
....
....
....
....
....
....
....
....
....
....
....
....
....
....
....
....
....
....
....
....
....
....
....
....
....

Was this dream... a recurring dream? a lucid dream? a nightmare?
 ☐ Yes ☐ No ☐ Yes ☐ No ☐ Yes ☐ No

What were the key themes or issues in the dream?

....
....
....

What were your prominent emotions and feelings?

☐ Happiness ☐ Surprise ☐ Indifference ☐ Fear ☐ Disapproval
☐ Love ☐ Joy ☐ Sadness ☐ Panic ☐ Rejection
☐ Freedom ☐ Contentment ☐ Frustration ☐ Envy ☐ Anxiety
☐ Compassion ☐ Pride ☐ Betrayal ☐ Jealousy ☐ Guilt
☐ Arousal ☐ Confusion ☐ Anger ☐ Shame ☐ Pain
Other? ☐ ☐
 ....
 ☐ ☐
 ....

Could this dream relate to a recent situation/event/person/problem in your life?

....
....
....

What is your interpretation of the dream?

....
....
....
....
....
....
....

In what way(s) does this dream affect you?
Does it provide clarity into something or suggest a specific course of action?

....
....
....

Dream title: _____   Date: _____

Dream description

....
....
....
....
....
....
....
....
....
....
....
....
....
....
....
....
....
....
....
....
....
....
....
....
....
....
....
....
....
....
....
....

Was this dream... a recurring dream? a lucid dream? a nightmare?
☐ Yes ☐ No ☐ Yes ☐ No ☐ Yes ☐ No

What were the key themes or issues in the dream?

....

....

....

What were your prominent emotions and feelings?

☐ Happiness	☐ Surprise	☐ Indifference	☐ Fear	☐ Disapproval
☐ Love	☐ Joy	☐ Sadness	☐ Panic	☐ Rejection
☐ Freedom	☐ Contentment	☐ Frustration	☐ Envy	☐ Anxiety
☐ Compassion	☐ Pride	☐ Betrayal	☐ Jealousy	☐ Guilt
☐ Arousal	☐ Confusion	☐ Anger	☐ Shame	☐ Pain

Other?
☐ .... ☐ ....
☐ .... ☐ ....

Could this dream relate to a recent situation/event/person/problem in your life?

....

....

....

What is your interpretation of the dream?

....

....

....

....

....

....

In what way(s) does this dream affect you?
Does it provide clarity into something or suggest a specific course of action?

....

....

....

Dream title: _____ Date: _____

Dream description

....
....
....
....
....
....
....
....
....
....
....
....
....
....
....
....
....
....
....
....
....
....
....
....
....
....
....
....
....
....

Was this dream... a recurring dream? a lucid dream? a nightmare?
 □ Yes □ No □ Yes □ No □ Yes □ No

What were the key themes or issues in the dream?

....

....

....

What were your prominent emotions and feelings?

□ Happiness	□ Surprise	□ Indifference	□ Fear	□ Disapproval
□ Love	□ Joy	□ Sadness	□ Panic	□ Rejection
□ Freedom	□ Contentment	□ Frustration	□ Envy	□ Anxiety
□ Compassion	□ Pride	□ Betrayal	□ Jealousy	□ Guilt
□ Arousal	□ Confusion	□ Anger	□ Shame	□ Pain

Other? □ .... □ ....

□ .... □ ....

Could this dream relate to a recent situation/event/person/problem in your life?

....

....

....

What is your interpretation of the dream?

....

....

....

....

....

....

....

In what way(s) does this dream affect you?
Does it provide clarity into something or suggest a specific course of action?

....

....

....

Dream title: _____ Date: _____

Dream description

....
....
....
....
....
....
....
....
....
....
....
....
....
....
....
....
....
....
....
....
....
....
....
....
....
....
....
....
....
....

Was this dream... a recurring dream? a lucid dream? a nightmare?
⬜ Yes ⬜ No ⬜ Yes ⬜ No ⬜ Yes ⬜ No

What were the key themes or issues in the dream?

....

....

....

What were your prominent emotions and feelings?

⬜ Happiness	⬜ Surprise	⬜ Indifference	⬜ Fear	⬜ Disapproval
⬜ Love	⬜ Joy	⬜ Sadness	⬜ Panic	⬜ Rejection
⬜ Freedom	⬜ Contentment	⬜ Frustration	⬜ Envy	⬜ Anxiety
⬜ Compassion	⬜ Pride	⬜ Betrayal	⬜ Jealousy	⬜ Guilt
⬜ Arousal	⬜ Confusion	⬜ Anger	⬜ Shame	⬜ Pain

Other?
⬜ .... ⬜ ....
⬜ .... ⬜ ....

Could this dream relate to a recent situation/event/person/problem in your life?

....

....

....

What is your interpretation of the dream?

....

....

....

....

....

....

....

In what way(s) does this dream affect you?
Does it provide clarity into something or suggest a specific course of action?

....

....

....

Dream title: Date:

Dream description

....
....
....
....
....
....
....
....
....
....
....
....
....
....
....
....
....
....
....
....
....
....
....
....
....
....
....
....
....
....

Was this dream...   a recurring dream?   a lucid dream?   a nightmare?

☐ Yes ☐ No   ☐ Yes ☐ No   ☐ Yes ☐ No

What were the key themes or issues in the dream?

....

....

....

What were your prominent emotions and feelings?

☐ Happiness   ☐ Surprise   ☐ Indifference   ☐ Fear   ☐ Disapproval

☐ Love   ☐ Joy   ☐ Sadness   ☐ Panic   ☐ Rejection

☐ Freedom   ☐ Contentment   ☐ Frustration   ☐ Envy   ☐ Anxiety

☐ Compassion   ☐ Pride   ☐ Betrayal   ☐ Jealousy   ☐ Guilt

☐ Arousal   ☐ Confusion   ☐ Anger   ☐ Shame   ☐ Pain

Other?   ☐ ....   ☐ ....

   ☐ ....   ☐ ....

Could this dream relate to a recent situation/event/person/problem in your life?

....

....

....

What is your interpretation of the dream?

....

....

....

....

....

....

....

In what way(s) does this dream affect you?
Does it provide clarity into something or suggest a specific course of action?

....

....

....

Dream title: _____   Date: _____

Dream description

....
....
....
....
....
....
....
....
....
....
....
....
....
....
....
....
....
....
....
....
....
....
....
....
....
....
....
....
....
....
....
....

Was this dream... a recurring dream? a lucid dream? a nightmare?
☐ Yes ☐ No ☐ Yes ☐ No ☐ Yes ☐ No

What were the key themes or issues in the dream?

....
....
....

What were your prominent emotions and feelings?

☐ Happiness	☐ Surprise	☐ Indifference	☐ Fear	☐ Disapproval
☐ Love	☐ Joy	☐ Sadness	☐ Panic	☐ Rejection
☐ Freedom	☐ Contentment	☐ Frustration	☐ Envy	☐ Anxiety
☐ Compassion	☐ Pride	☐ Betrayal	☐ Jealousy	☐ Guilt
☐ Arousal	☐ Confusion	☐ Anger	☐ Shame	☐ Pain
Other?	☐		☐	
	☐		☐	

Could this dream relate to a recent situation/event/person/problem in your life?

....
....
....

What is your interpretation of the dream?

....
....
....
....
....
....
....

In what way(s) does this dream affect you?
Does it provide clarity into something or suggest a specific course of action?

....
....
....

Dream title: _____ Date: _____

Dream description

....
....
....
....
....
....
....
....
....
....
....
....
....
....
....
....
....
....
....
....
....
....
....
....
....
....
....
....
....
....
....

Was this dream...   a recurring dream?   a lucid dream?   a nightmare?
　　　　　　　　　　　☐ Yes ☐ No   ☐ Yes ☐ No   ☐ Yes ☐ No

What were the key themes or issues in the dream?

....
....
....

What were your prominent emotions and feelings?

☐ Happiness	☐ Surprise	☐ Indifference	☐ Fear	☐ Disapproval
☐ Love	☐ Joy	☐ Sadness	☐ Panic	☐ Rejection
☐ Freedom	☐ Contentment	☐ Frustration	☐ Envy	☐ Anxiety
☐ Compassion	☐ Pride	☐ Betrayal	☐ Jealousy	☐ Guilt
☐ Arousal	☐ Confusion	☐ Anger	☐ Shame	☐ Pain
Other?	☐		☐	
	☐		☐	

Could this dream relate to a recent situation/event/person/problem in your life?

....
....
....

What is your interpretation of the dream?

....
....
....
....
....
....
....

In what way(s) does this dream affect you?
Does it provide clarity into something or suggest a specific course of action?

....
....
....

Dream title: _____ Date: _____

Dream description

....
....
....
....
....
....
....
....
....
....
....
....
....
....
....
....
....
....
....
....
....
....
....
....
....
....
....
....
....
....

Was this dream...   a recurring dream?   a lucid dream?   a nightmare?
                        ☐ Yes ☐ No   ☐ Yes ☐ No   ☐ Yes ☐ No

What were the key themes or issues in the dream?

....

....

....

What were your prominent emotions and feelings?

☐ Happiness	☐ Surprise	☐ Indifference	☐ Fear	☐ Disapproval
☐ Love	☐ Joy	☐ Sadness	☐ Panic	☐ Rejection
☐ Freedom	☐ Contentment	☐ Frustration	☐ Envy	☐ Anxiety
☐ Compassion	☐ Pride	☐ Betrayal	☐ Jealousy	☐ Guilt
☐ Arousal	☐ Confusion	☐ Anger	☐ Shame	☐ Pain

Other?   ☐ ....   ☐ ....

        ☐ ....   ☐ ....

Could this dream relate to a recent situation/event/person/problem in your life?

....

....

....

What is your interpretation of the dream?

....

....

....

....

....

....

In what way(s) does this dream affect you?
Does it provide clarity into something or suggest a specific course of action?

....

....

....

Dream title: _____   Date: _____

Dream description

....
....
....
....
....
....
....
....
....
....
....
....
....
....
....
....
....
....
....
....
....
....
....
....
....
....
....
....
....
....
....

Was this dream...   a recurring dream?   a lucid dream?   a nightmare?
                    ☐ Yes ☐ No   ☐ Yes ☐ No   ☐ Yes ☐ No

What were the key themes or issues in the dream?

....

....

....

What were your prominent emotions and feelings?

☐ Happiness	☐ Surprise	☐ Indifference	☐ Fear	☐ Disapproval
☐ Love	☐ Joy	☐ Sadness	☐ Panic	☐ Rejection
☐ Freedom	☐ Contentment	☐ Frustration	☐ Envy	☐ Anxiety
☐ Compassion	☐ Pride	☐ Betrayal	☐ Jealousy	☐ Guilt
☐ Arousal	☐ Confusion	☐ Anger	☐ Shame	☐ Pain

Other?   ☐ ....   ☐ ....
         ☐ ....   ☐ ....

Could this dream relate to a recent situation/event/person/problem in your life?

....

....

....

What is your interpretation of the dream?

....

....

....

....

....

....

....

In what way(s) does this dream affect you?
Does it provide clarity into something or suggest a specific course of action?

....

....

....

Dream title: Date:

Dream description

Was this dream...   a recurring dream?   a lucid dream?   a nightmare?
                           ☐ Yes ☐ No   ☐ Yes ☐ No   ☐ Yes ☐ No

What were the key themes or issues in the dream?

....

....

....

What were your prominent emotions and feelings?

☐ Happiness	☐ Surprise	☐ Indifference	☐ Fear	☐ Disapproval
☐ Love	☐ Joy	☐ Sadness	☐ Panic	☐ Rejection
☐ Freedom	☐ Contentment	☐ Frustration	☐ Envy	☐ Anxiety
☐ Compassion	☐ Pride	☐ Betrayal	☐ Jealousy	☐ Guilt
☐ Arousal	☐ Confusion	☐ Anger	☐ Shame	☐ Pain

Other?   ☐ ....   ☐ ....

              ☐ ....   ☐ ....

Could this dream relate to a recent situation/event/person/problem in your life?

....

....

....

What is your interpretation of the dream?

....

....

....

....

....

....

....

In what way(s) does this dream affect you?
Does it provide clarity into something or suggest a specific course of action?

....

....

....

Dream title: _____   Date: _____

Dream description

....
....
....
....
....
....
....
....
....
....
....
....
....
....
....
....
....
....
....
....
....
....
....
....
....
....
....
....
....
....

Was this dream...   a recurring dream?   a lucid dream?   a nightmare?
                     ☐ Yes ☐ No   ☐ Yes ☐ No   ☐ Yes ☐ No

What were the key themes or issues in the dream?

....

....

....

What were your prominent emotions and feelings?

☐ Happiness	☐ Surprise	☐ Indifference	☐ Fear	☐ Disapproval
☐ Love	☐ Joy	☐ Sadness	☐ Panic	☐ Rejection
☐ Freedom	☐ Contentment	☐ Frustration	☐ Envy	☐ Anxiety
☐ Compassion	☐ Pride	☐ Betrayal	☐ Jealousy	☐ Guilt
☐ Arousal	☐ Confusion	☐ Anger	☐ Shame	☐ Pain

Other?   ☐ ....   ☐ ....

          ☐ ....   ☐ ....

Could this dream relate to a recent situation/event/person/problem in your life?

....

....

....

What is your interpretation of the dream?

....

....

....

....

....

....

....

In what way(s) does this dream affect you?
Does it provide clarity into something or suggest a specific course of action?

....

....

....

Dream title: _____ Date: _____

_____

Dream description
_____

....
....
....
....
....
....
....
....
....
....
....
....
....
....
....
....
....
....
....
....
....
....
....
....
....
....
....
....
....
....
....
....
....

Was this dream... a recurring dream? a lucid dream? a nightmare?
☐ Yes ☐ No ☐ Yes ☐ No ☐ Yes ☐ No

What were the key themes or issues in the dream?

....

....

....

What were your prominent emotions and feelings?

☐ Happiness	☐ Surprise	☐ Indifference	☐ Fear	☐ Disapproval
☐ Love	☐ Joy	☐ Sadness	☐ Panic	☐ Rejection
☐ Freedom	☐ Contentment	☐ Frustration	☐ Envy	☐ Anxiety
☐ Compassion	☐ Pride	☐ Betrayal	☐ Jealousy	☐ Guilt
☐ Arousal	☐ Confusion	☐ Anger	☐ Shame	☐ Pain

Other? ☐ .... ☐ ....

☐ .... ☐ ....

Could this dream relate to a recent situation/event/person/problem in your life?

....

....

....

What is your interpretation of the dream?

....

....

....

....

....

....

....

In what way(s) does this dream affect you?
Does it provide clarity into something or suggest a specific course of action?

....

....

....

Dream title: Date:

Dream description

....
....
....
....
....
....
....
....
....
....
....
....
....
....
....
....
....
....
....
....
....
....
....
....
....
....
....
....
....
....

Was this dream... a recurring dream? a lucid dream? a nightmare?
☐ Yes ☐ No ☐ Yes ☐ No ☐ Yes ☐ No

What were the key themes or issues in the dream?

....
....
....

What were your prominent emotions and feelings?

☐ Happiness	☐ Surprise	☐ Indifference	☐ Fear	☐ Disapproval
☐ Love	☐ Joy	☐ Sadness	☐ Panic	☐ Rejection
☐ Freedom	☐ Contentment	☐ Frustration	☐ Envy	☐ Anxiety
☐ Compassion	☐ Pride	☐ Betrayal	☐ Jealousy	☐ Guilt
☐ Arousal	☐ Confusion	☐ Anger	☐ Shame	☐ Pain

Other? ☐ .... ☐ ....
☐ .... ☐ ....

Could this dream relate to a recent situation/event/person/problem in your life?

....
....
....

What is your interpretation of the dream?

....
....
....
....
....
....
....

In what way(s) does this dream affect you?
Does it provide clarity into something or suggest a specific course of action?

....
....
....

Dream title: _____ Date: _____

Dream description

....
....
....
....
....
....
....
....
....
....
....
....
....
....
....
....
....
....
....
....
....
....
....
....
....
....
....
....
....
....
....

Was this dream... a recurring dream? a lucid dream? a nightmare?
☐ Yes ☐ No ☐ Yes ☐ No ☐ Yes ☐ No

What were the key themes or issues in the dream?

....

....

....

What were your prominent emotions and feelings?

☐ Happiness	☐ Surprise	☐ Indifference	☐ Fear	☐ Disapproval
☐ Love	☐ Joy	☐ Sadness	☐ Panic	☐ Rejection
☐ Freedom	☐ Contentment	☐ Frustration	☐ Envy	☐ Anxiety
☐ Compassion	☐ Pride	☐ Betrayal	☐ Jealousy	☐ Guilt
☐ Arousal	☐ Confusion	☐ Anger	☐ Shame	☐ Pain

Other? ☐ .... ☐ ....
        ☐ .... ☐ ....

Could this dream relate to a recent situation/event/person/problem in your life?

....

....

....

What is your interpretation of the dream?

....

....

....

....

....

....

In what way(s) does this dream affect you?
Does it provide clarity into something or suggest a specific course of action?

....

....

....

Dream title: _____ Date: _____

Dream description

....
....
....
....
....
....
....
....
....
....
....
....
....
....
....
....
....
....
....
....
....
....
....
....
....
....
....
....
....
....

Was this dream... a recurring dream? a lucid dream? a nightmare?
     ☐ Yes ☐ No   ☐ Yes ☐ No   ☐ Yes ☐ No

What were the key themes or issues in the dream?

....

....

....

What were your prominent emotions and feelings?

☐ Happiness   ☐ Surprise   ☐ Indifference   ☐ Fear   ☐ Disapproval

☐ Love   ☐ Joy   ☐ Sadness   ☐ Panic   ☐ Rejection

☐ Freedom   ☐ Contentment   ☐ Frustration   ☐ Envy   ☐ Anxiety

☐ Compassion   ☐ Pride   ☐ Betrayal   ☐ Jealousy   ☐ Guilt

☐ Arousal   ☐ Confusion   ☐ Anger   ☐ Shame   ☐ Pain

Other?   ☐ ....   ☐ ....

      ☐ ....   ☐ ....

Could this dream relate to a recent situation/event/person/problem in your life?

....

....

....

What is your interpretation of the dream?

....

....

....

....

....

....

....

In what way(s) does this dream affect you?
Does it provide clarity into something or suggest a specific course of action?

....

....

....

Dream title: _____ Date: _____

Dream description

....
....
....
....
....
....
....
....
....
....
....
....
....
....
....
....
....
....
....
....
....
....
....
....
....
....
....
....
....
....
....
....

Was this dream...   a recurring dream?   a lucid dream?   a nightmare?
 ☐ Yes ☐ No   ☐ Yes ☐ No   ☐ Yes ☐ No

What were the key themes or issues in the dream?

....
....
....

What were your prominent emotions and feelings?

☐ Happiness	☐ Surprise	☐ Indifference	☐ Fear	☐ Disapproval
☐ Love	☐ Joy	☐ Sadness	☐ Panic	☐ Rejection
☐ Freedom	☐ Contentment	☐ Frustration	☐ Envy	☐ Anxiety
☐ Compassion	☐ Pride	☐ Betrayal	☐ Jealousy	☐ Guilt
☐ Arousal	☐ Confusion	☐ Anger	☐ Shame	☐ Pain

Other?
 ☐ .... ☐ ....
 ☐ .... ☐ ....

Could this dream relate to a recent situation/event/person/problem in your life?

....
....
....

What is your interpretation of the dream?

....
....
....
....
....
....
....

In what way(s) does this dream affect you?
Does it provide clarity into something or suggest a specific course of action?

....
....
....

Dream title: Date:

Dream description

....

....

....

....

....

....

....

....

....

....

....

....

....

....

....

....

....

....

....

....

....

....

....

....

....

....

....

....

Was this dream...   a recurring dream?   a lucid dream?   a nightmare?
                         ☐ Yes ☐ No   ☐ Yes ☐ No   ☐ Yes ☐ No

What were the key themes or issues in the dream?

....

....

....

What were your prominent emotions and feelings?

☐ Happiness   ☐ Surprise   ☐ Indifference   ☐ Fear   ☐ Disapproval

☐ Love   ☐ Joy   ☐ Sadness   ☐ Panic   ☐ Rejection

☐ Freedom   ☐ Contentment   ☐ Frustration   ☐ Envy   ☐ Anxiety

☐ Compassion   ☐ Pride   ☐ Betrayal   ☐ Jealousy   ☐ Guilt

☐ Arousal   ☐ Confusion   ☐ Anger   ☐ Shame   ☐ Pain

Other?   ☐   ☐
                 ....
                 ☐   ☐
                 ....

Could this dream relate to a recent situation/event/person/problem in your life?

....

....

....

What is your interpretation of the dream?

....

....

....

....

....

....

In what way(s) does this dream affect you?
Does it provide clarity into something or suggest a specific course of action?

....

....

....

Dream title: _____   Date: _____

Dream description

....

....

....

....

....

....

....

....

....

....

....

....

....

....

....

....

....

....

....

....

....

....

....

....

....

....

....

....

....

....

Was this dream...
a recurring dream?
☐ Yes ☐ No
a lucid dream?
☐ Yes ☐ No
a nightmare?
☐ Yes ☐ No

What were the key themes or issues in the dream?

....

....

....

What were your prominent emotions and feelings?

☐ Happiness	☐ Surprise	☐ Indifference	☐ Fear	☐ Disapproval
☐ Love	☐ Joy	☐ Sadness	☐ Panic	☐ Rejection
☐ Freedom	☐ Contentment	☐ Frustration	☐ Envy	☐ Anxiety
☐ Compassion	☐ Pride	☐ Betrayal	☐ Jealousy	☐ Guilt
☐ Arousal	☐ Confusion	☐ Anger	☐ Shame	☐ Pain

Other? ☐ .... ☐ ....

☐ .... ☐ ....

Could this dream relate to a recent situation/event/person/problem in your life?

....

....

....

What is your interpretation of the dream?

....

....

....

....

....

....

....

In what way(s) does this dream affect you?
Does it provide clarity into something or suggest a specific course of action?

....

....

....

Dream title: _____ Date: _____

Dream description

···
···
···
···
···
···
···
···
···
···
···
···
···
···
···
···
···
···
···
···
···
···
···
···
···
···
···
···
···
···

Was this dream... a recurring dream?   a lucid dream?   a nightmare?
☐ Yes ☐ No   ☐ Yes ☐ No   ☐ Yes ☐ No

What were the key themes or issues in the dream?

....

....

....

What were your prominent emotions and feelings?

☐ Happiness	☐ Surprise	☐ Indifference	☐ Fear	☐ Disapproval
☐ Love	☐ Joy	☐ Sadness	☐ Panic	☐ Rejection
☐ Freedom	☐ Contentment	☐ Frustration	☐ Envy	☐ Anxiety
☐ Compassion	☐ Pride	☐ Betrayal	☐ Jealousy	☐ Guilt
☐ Arousal	☐ Confusion	☐ Anger	☐ Shame	☐ Pain

Other?   ☐ ....   ☐ ....

         ☐ ....   ☐ ....

Could this dream relate to a recent situation/event/person/problem in your life?

....

....

....

What is your interpretation of the dream?

....

....

....

....

....

....

....

In what way(s) does this dream affect you?
Does it provide clarity into something or suggest a specific course of action?

....

....

....

Dream title: _____ Date: _____

Dream description

....
....
....
....
....
....
....
....
....
....
....
....
....
....
....
....
....
....
....
....
....
....
....
....
....
....
....
....
....
....
....

Was this dream...   a recurring dream?   a lucid dream?   a nightmare?
☐ Yes   ☐ No   ☐ Yes   ☐ No   ☐ Yes   ☐ No

What were the key themes or issues in the dream?

....
....
....

What were your prominent emotions and feelings?

☐ Happiness	☐ Surprise	☐ Indifference	☐ Fear	☐ Disapproval
☐ Love	☐ Joy	☐ Sadness	☐ Panic	☐ Rejection
☐ Freedom	☐ Contentment	☐ Frustration	☐ Envy	☐ Anxiety
☐ Compassion	☐ Pride	☐ Betrayal	☐ Jealousy	☐ Guilt
☐ Arousal	☐ Confusion	☐ Anger	☐ Shame	☐ Pain

Other?
☐ ....   ☐ ....
☐ ....   ☐ ....

Could this dream relate to a recent situation/event/person/problem in your life?

....
....
....

What is your interpretation of the dream?

....
....
....
....
....
....
....

In what way(s) does this dream affect you?
Does it provide clarity into something or suggest a specific course of action?

....
....
....

Dream title: Date:

Dream description

....
....
....
....
....
....
....
....
....
....
....
....
....
....
....
....
....
....
....
....
....
....
....
....
....
....
....
....
....
....

Was this dream... a recurring dream? a lucid dream? a nightmare?
                   ☐ Yes ☐ No   ☐ Yes ☐ No   ☐ Yes ☐ No

What were the key themes or issues in the dream?

....
....
....

What were your prominent emotions and feelings?

☐ Happiness	☐ Surprise	☐ Indifference	☐ Fear	☐ Disapproval
☐ Love	☐ Joy	☐ Sadness	☐ Panic	☐ Rejection
☐ Freedom	☐ Contentment	☐ Frustration	☐ Envy	☐ Anxiety
☐ Compassion	☐ Pride	☐ Betrayal	☐ Jealousy	☐ Guilt
☐ Arousal	☐ Confusion	☐ Anger	☐ Shame	☐ Pain

Other?   ☐ ....   ☐ ....
         ☐ ....   ☐ ....

Could this dream relate to a recent situation/event/person/problem in your life?

....
....
....

What is your interpretation of the dream?

....
....
....
....
....
....

In what way(s) does this dream affect you?
Does it provide clarity into something or suggest a specific course of action?

....
....
....

Dream title: Date:

Dream description

....

....

....

....

....

....

....

....

....

....

....

....

....

....

....

....

....

....

....

....

....

....

....

....

....

....

....

....

Was this dream...   a recurring dream?   a lucid dream?   a nightmare?

☐ Yes ☐ No   ☐ Yes ☐ No   ☐ Yes ☐ No

What were the key themes or issues in the dream?

....

....

....

What were your prominent emotions and feelings?

☐ Happiness	☐ Surprise	☐ Indifference	☐ Fear	☐ Disapproval
☐ Love	☐ Joy	☐ Sadness	☐ Panic	☐ Rejection
☐ Freedom	☐ Contentment	☐ Frustration	☐ Envy	☐ Anxiety
☐ Compassion	☐ Pride	☐ Betrayal	☐ Jealousy	☐ Guilt
☐ Arousal	☐ Confusion	☐ Anger	☐ Shame	☐ Pain

Other?   ☐ ....   ☐ ....

       ☐ ....   ☐ ....

Could this dream relate to a recent situation/event/person/problem in your life?

....

....

....

What is your interpretation of the dream?

....

....

....

....

....

....

....

In what way(s) does this dream affect you?
Does it provide clarity into something or suggest a specific course of action?

....

....

....

Dream title: _____ Date: _____

Dream description

....
....
....
....
....
....
....
....
....
....
....
....
....
....
....
....
....
....
....
....
....
....
....
....
....
....
....
....
....
....
....
....
....
....

Was this dream...   a recurring dream?   a lucid dream?   a nightmare?
                       ☐ Yes ☐ No   ☐ Yes ☐ No   ☐ Yes ☐ No

What were the key themes or issues in the dream?

....

....

....

What were your prominent emotions and feelings?

☐ Happiness	☐ Surprise	☐ Indifference	☐ Fear	☐ Disapproval
☐ Love	☐ Joy	☐ Sadness	☐ Panic	☐ Rejection
☐ Freedom	☐ Contentment	☐ Frustration	☐ Envy	☐ Anxiety
☐ Compassion	☐ Pride	☐ Betrayal	☐ Jealousy	☐ Guilt
☐ Arousal	☐ Confusion	☐ Anger	☐ Shame	☐ Pain
Other?	☐		☐	
	☐		☐	

Could this dream relate to a recent situation/event/person/problem in your life?

....

....

....

What is your interpretation of the dream?

....

....

....

....

....

....

....

In what way(s) does this dream affect you?
Does it provide clarity into something or suggest a specific course of action?

....

....

....

Dream title: _____   Date: _____

Dream description

....
....
....
....
....
....
....
....
....
....
....
....
....
....
....
....
....
....
....
....
....
....
....
....
....
....
....
....
....
....

Was this dream... a recurring dream? a lucid dream? a nightmare?
☐ Yes ☐ No ☐ Yes ☐ No ☐ Yes ☐ No

What were the key themes or issues in the dream?

....
....
....

What were your prominent emotions and feelings?

☐ Happiness ☐ Surprise ☐ Indifference ☐ Fear ☐ Disapproval
☐ Love ☐ Joy ☐ Sadness ☐ Panic ☐ Rejection
☐ Freedom ☐ Contentment ☐ Frustration ☐ Envy ☐ Anxiety
☐ Compassion ☐ Pride ☐ Betrayal ☐ Jealousy ☐ Guilt
☐ Arousal ☐ Confusion ☐ Anger ☐ Shame ☐ Pain
Other? ☐ .... ☐ ....
☐ .... ☐ ....

Could this dream relate to a recent situation/event/person/problem in your life?

....
....
....

What is your interpretation of the dream?

....
....
....
....
....
....
....

In what way(s) does this dream affect you?
Does it provide clarity into something or suggest a specific course of action?

....
....
....

Dream title: _____ Date: _____

Dream description

....
....
....
....
....
....
....
....
....
....
....
....
....
....
....
....
....
....
....
....
....
....
....
....
....
....
....
....
....
....
....
....
....
....

Was this dream...   a recurring dream?   a lucid dream?   a nightmare?
☐ Yes ☐ No   ☐ Yes ☐ No   ☐ Yes ☐ No

What were the key themes or issues in the dream?

....
....
....

What were your prominent emotions and feelings?

☐ Happiness	☐ Surprise	☐ Indifference	☐ Fear	☐ Disapproval
☐ Love	☐ Joy	☐ Sadness	☐ Panic	☐ Rejection
☐ Freedom	☐ Contentment	☐ Frustration	☐ Envy	☐ Anxiety
☐ Compassion	☐ Pride	☐ Betrayal	☐ Jealousy	☐ Guilt
☐ Arousal	☐ Confusion	☐ Anger	☐ Shame	☐ Pain

Other?   ☐ ....   ☐ ....
          ☐ ....   ☐ ....

Could this dream relate to a recent situation/event/person/problem in your life?

....
....
....

What is your interpretation of the dream?

....
....
....
....
....
....
....

In what way(s) does this dream affect you?
Does it provide clarity into something or suggest a specific course of action?

....
....
....

Dream title: _____ Date: _____

Dream description

....
....
....
....
....
....
....
....
....
....
....
....
....
....
....
....
....
....
....
....
....
....
....
....
....
....
....
....
....
....
....
....
....

Was this dream...   a recurring dream?   a lucid dream?   a nightmare?
☐ Yes ☐ No   ☐ Yes ☐ No   ☐ Yes ☐ No

What were the key themes or issues in the dream?

....

....

....

What were your prominent emotions and feelings?

☐ Happiness	☐ Surprise	☐ Indifference	☐ Fear	☐ Disapproval
☐ Love	☐ Joy	☐ Sadness	☐ Panic	☐ Rejection
☐ Freedom	☐ Contentment	☐ Frustration	☐ Envy	☐ Anxiety
☐ Compassion	☐ Pride	☐ Betrayal	☐ Jealousy	☐ Guilt
☐ Arousal	☐ Confusion	☐ Anger	☐ Shame	☐ Pain

Other?   ☐ ....   ☐ ....

☐ ....   ☐ ....

Could this dream relate to a recent situation/event/person/problem in your life?

....

....

....

What is your interpretation of the dream?

....

....

....

....

....

....

....

In what way(s) does this dream affect you?
Does it provide clarity into something or suggest a specific course of action?

....

....

....

Dream title: _____   Date: _____

Dream description

....
....
....
....
....
....
....
....
....
....
....
....
....
....
....
....
....
....
....
....
....
....
....
....
....
....
....
....
....
....

Was this dream...   a recurring dream?   a lucid dream?   a nightmare?
☐ Yes ☐ No   ☐ Yes ☐ No   ☐ Yes ☐ No

What were the key themes or issues in the dream?

....

....

....

What were your prominent emotions and feelings?

☐ Happiness	☐ Surprise	☐ Indifference	☐ Fear	☐ Disapproval
☐ Love	☐ Joy	☐ Sadness	☐ Panic	☐ Rejection
☐ Freedom	☐ Contentment	☐ Frustration	☐ Envy	☐ Anxiety
☐ Compassion	☐ Pride	☐ Betrayal	☐ Jealousy	☐ Guilt
☐ Arousal	☐ Confusion	☐ Anger	☐ Shame	☐ Pain

Other?   ☐ ....   ☐ ....

☐ ....   ☐ ....

Could this dream relate to a recent situation/event/person/problem in your life?

....

....

....

What is your interpretation of the dream?

....

....

....

....

....

....

....

In what way(s) does this dream affect you?
Does it provide clarity into something or suggest a specific course of action?

....

....

....

Dream title: Date:

Dream description

Was this dream... | a recurring dream? | a lucid dream? | a nightmare?

☐ Yes ☐ No ☐ Yes ☐ No ☐ Yes ☐ No

What were the key themes or issues in the dream?

....

....

....

What were your prominent emotions and feelings?

☐ Happiness ☐ Surprise ☐ Indifference ☐ Fear ☐ Disapproval

☐ Love ☐ Joy ☐ Sadness ☐ Panic ☐ Rejection

☐ Freedom ☐ Contentment ☐ Frustration ☐ Envy ☐ Anxiety

☐ Compassion ☐ Pride ☐ Betrayal ☐ Jealousy ☐ Guilt

☐ Arousal ☐ Confusion ☐ Anger ☐ Shame ☐ Pain

Other? ☐ .... ☐ ....

☐ .... ☐ ....

Could this dream relate to a recent situation/event/person/problem in your life?

....

....

....

What is your interpretation of the dream?

....

....

....

....

....

....

....

In what way(s) does this dream affect you?
Does it provide clarity into something or suggest a specific course of action?

....

....

....

Dream title: _____ Date: _____

Dream description

Was this dream...   a recurring dream?   a lucid dream?   a nightmare?
                         ☐ Yes ☐ No   ☐ Yes ☐ No   ☐ Yes ☐ No

What were the key themes or issues in the dream?

....

....

....

What were your prominent emotions and feelings?

☐ Happiness   ☐ Surprise   ☐ Indifference   ☐ Fear   ☐ Disapproval

☐ Love   ☐ Joy   ☐ Sadness   ☐ Panic   ☐ Rejection

☐ Freedom   ☐ Contentment   ☐ Frustration   ☐ Envy   ☐ Anxiety

☐ Compassion   ☐ Pride   ☐ Betrayal   ☐ Jealousy   ☐ Guilt

☐ Arousal   ☐ Confusion   ☐ Anger   ☐ Shame   ☐ Pain

Other?   ☐ ....   ☐ ....

        ☐ ....   ☐ ....

Could this dream relate to a recent situation/event/person/problem in your life?

....

....

....

What is your interpretation of the dream?

....

....

....

....

....

....

....

In what way(s) does this dream affect you?
Does it provide clarity into something or suggest a specific course of action?

....

....

....

Dream title: _____   Date: _____

Dream description

....
....
....
....
....
....
....
....
....
....
....
....
....
....
....
....
....
....
....
....
....
....
....
....
....
....
....

Was this dream...
a recurring dream?	a lucid dream?	a nightmare?
☐ Yes ☐ No	☐ Yes ☐ No	☐ Yes ☐ No

What were the key themes or issues in the dream?

....

....

....

What were your prominent emotions and feelings?

☐ Happiness	☐ Surprise	☐ Indifference	☐ Fear	☐ Disapproval
☐ Love	☐ Joy	☐ Sadness	☐ Panic	☐ Rejection
☐ Freedom	☐ Contentment	☐ Frustration	☐ Envy	☐ Anxiety
☐ Compassion	☐ Pride	☐ Betrayal	☐ Jealousy	☐ Guilt
☐ Arousal	☐ Confusion	☐ Anger	☐ Shame	☐ Pain

Other?
☐ ....   ☐ ....
☐ ....   ☐ ....

Could this dream relate to a recent situation/event/person/problem in your life?

....

....

....

What is your interpretation of the dream?

....

....

....

....

....

....

In what way(s) does this dream affect you?
Does it provide clarity into something or suggest a specific course of action?

....

....

....

Dream title: _____ Date: _____

Dream description

....
....
....
....
....
....
....
....
....
....
....
....
....
....
....
....
....
....
....
....
....
....
....
....
....
....
....
....
....
....
....

Was this dream... a recurring dream? a lucid dream? a nightmare?
                   ☐ Yes ☐ No   ☐ Yes ☐ No   ☐ Yes ☐ No

What were the key themes or issues in the dream?

....

....

....

What were your prominent emotions and feelings?

☐ Happiness	☐ Surprise	☐ Indifference	☐ Fear	☐ Disapproval
☐ Love	☐ Joy	☐ Sadness	☐ Panic	☐ Rejection
☐ Freedom	☐ Contentment	☐ Frustration	☐ Envy	☐ Anxiety
☐ Compassion	☐ Pride	☐ Betrayal	☐ Jealousy	☐ Guilt
☐ Arousal	☐ Confusion	☐ Anger	☐ Shame	☐ Pain

Other? ☐ .... ☐ ....

☐ .... ☐ ....

Could this dream relate to a recent situation/event/person/problem in your life?

....

....

....

What is your interpretation of the dream?

....

....

....

....

....

....

....

In what way(s) does this dream affect you?
Does it provide clarity into something or suggest a specific course of action?

....

....

....

Dream title: _____ Date: _____

Dream description

....
....
....
....
....
....
....
....
....
....
....
....
....
....
....
....
....
....
....
....
....
....
....
....
....
....
....
....
....
....
....

Was this dream...   a recurring dream?   a lucid dream?   a nightmare?
                     ☐ Yes ☐ No   ☐ Yes ☐ No   ☐ Yes ☐ No

What were the key themes or issues in the dream?

....
....
....

What were your prominent emotions and feelings?

☐ Happiness   ☐ Surprise   ☐ Indifference   ☐ Fear   ☐ Disapproval
☐ Love   ☐ Joy   ☐ Sadness   ☐ Panic   ☐ Rejection
☐ Freedom   ☐ Contentment   ☐ Frustration   ☐ Envy   ☐ Anxiety
☐ Compassion   ☐ Pride   ☐ Betrayal   ☐ Jealousy   ☐ Guilt
☐ Arousal   ☐ Confusion   ☐ Anger   ☐ Shame   ☐ Pain
Other?   ☐ ....   ☐ ....
               ☐ ....   ☐ ....

Could this dream relate to a recent situation/event/person/problem in your life?

....
....
....

What is your interpretation of the dream?

....
....
....
....
....
....
....

In what way(s) does this dream affect you?
Does it provide clarity into something or suggest a specific course of action?

....
....
....

Dream title: _____ Date: _____

Dream description

....
....
....
....
....
....
....
....
....
....
....
....
....
....
....
....
....
....
....
....
....
....
....
....
....
....
....
....
....
....
....

Was this dream... a recurring dream? a lucid dream? a nightmare?
☐ Yes ☐ No ☐ Yes ☐ No ☐ Yes ☐ No

What were the key themes or issues in the dream?

....
....
....

What were your prominent emotions and feelings?

☐ Happiness	☐ Surprise	☐ Indifference	☐ Fear	☐ Disapproval
☐ Love	☐ Joy	☐ Sadness	☐ Panic	☐ Rejection
☐ Freedom	☐ Contentment	☐ Frustration	☐ Envy	☐ Anxiety
☐ Compassion	☐ Pride	☐ Betrayal	☐ Jealousy	☐ Guilt
☐ Arousal	☐ Confusion	☐ Anger	☐ Shame	☐ Pain
Other?	☐		☐	
	☐		☐	

Could this dream relate to a recent situation/event/person/problem in your life?

....
....
....

What is your interpretation of the dream?

....
....
....
....
....
....
....

In what way(s) does this dream affect you?
Does it provide clarity into something or suggest a specific course of action?

....
....
....

Dream title: _____ Date: _____

Dream description

....
....
....
....
....
....
....
....
....
....
....
....
....
....
....
....
....
....
....
....
....
....
....
....
....
....
....
....
....
....
....

Was this dream... a recurring dream? a lucid dream? a nightmare?

☐ Yes ☐ No   ☐ Yes ☐ No   ☐ Yes ☐ No

What were the key themes or issues in the dream?

....
....
....

What were your prominent emotions and feelings?

☐ Happiness	☐ Surprise	☐ Indifference	☐ Fear	☐ Disapproval
☐ Love	☐ Joy	☐ Sadness	☐ Panic	☐ Rejection
☐ Freedom	☐ Contentment	☐ Frustration	☐ Envy	☐ Anxiety
☐ Compassion	☐ Pride	☐ Betrayal	☐ Jealousy	☐ Guilt
☐ Arousal	☐ Confusion	☐ Anger	☐ Shame	☐ Pain

Other?   ☐ ....   ☐ ....

☐ ....   ☐ ....

Could this dream relate to a recent situation/event/person/problem in your life?

....
....
....

What is your interpretation of the dream?

....
....
....
....
....
....
....

In what way(s) does this dream affect you?
Does it provide clarity into something or suggest a specific course of action?

....
....
....

Dream title: _____ Date: _____

Dream description

....
....
....
....
....
....
....
....
....
....
....
....
....
....
....
....
....
....
....
....
....
....
....
....
....
....
....
....
....
....

Was this dream...   a recurring dream?   a lucid dream?   a nightmare?
☐ Yes   ☐ No   ☐ Yes   ☐ No   ☐ Yes   ☐ No

What were the key themes or issues in the dream?

....

....

....

What were your prominent emotions and feelings?

☐ Happiness   ☐ Surprise   ☐ Indifference   ☐ Fear   ☐ Disapproval
☐ Love   ☐ Joy   ☐ Sadness   ☐ Panic   ☐ Rejection
☐ Freedom   ☐ Contentment   ☐ Frustration   ☐ Envy   ☐ Anxiety
☐ Compassion   ☐ Pride   ☐ Betrayal   ☐ Jealousy   ☐ Guilt
☐ Arousal   ☐ Confusion   ☐ Anger   ☐ Shame   ☐ Pain
Other?   ☐ ....   ☐ ....
                ☐ ....   ☐ ....

Could this dream relate to a recent situation/event/person/problem in your life?

....

....

....

What is your interpretation of the dream?

....

....

....

....

....

....

....

In what way(s) does this dream affect you?
Does it provide clarity into something or suggest a specific course of action?

....

....

....

Dream title: _____   Date: _____

Dream description

....
....
....
....
....
....
....
....
....
....
....
....
....
....
....
....
....
....
....
....
....
....
....
....
....
....
....
....
....

Was this dream...　　a recurring dream?　　a lucid dream?　　a nightmare?
　　　　　　　　　　　☐ Yes　☐ No　　　☐ Yes　☐ No　　　☐ Yes　☐ No

What were the key themes or issues in the dream?

....

....

....

What were your prominent emotions and feelings?

☐ Happiness	☐ Surprise	☐ Indifference	☐ Fear	☐ Disapproval
☐ Love	☐ Joy	☐ Sadness	☐ Panic	☐ Rejection
☐ Freedom	☐ Contentment	☐ Frustration	☐ Envy	☐ Anxiety
☐ Compassion	☐ Pride	☐ Betrayal	☐ Jealousy	☐ Guilt
☐ Arousal	☐ Confusion	☐ Anger	☐ Shame	☐ Pain

Other?　☐ ....　☐ ....

☐ ....　☐ ....

Could this dream relate to a recent situation/event/person/problem in your life?

....

....

....

What is your interpretation of the dream?

....

....

....

....

....

....

....

In what way(s) does this dream affect you?
Does it provide clarity into something or suggest a specific course of action?

....

....

....

Dream title: Date:

Dream description

Was this dream...　　a recurring dream?　　a lucid dream?　　a nightmare?
　　　　　　　　　　☐ Yes　☐ No　　☐ Yes　☐ No　　☐ Yes　☐ No

What were the key themes or issues in the dream?

....

....

....

What were your prominent emotions and feelings?

☐ Happiness	☐ Surprise	☐ Indifference	☐ Fear	☐ Disapproval
☐ Love	☐ Joy	☐ Sadness	☐ Panic	☐ Rejection
☐ Freedom	☐ Contentment	☐ Frustration	☐ Envy	☐ Anxiety
☐ Compassion	☐ Pride	☐ Betrayal	☐ Jealousy	☐ Guilt
☐ Arousal	☐ Confusion	☐ Anger	☐ Shame	☐ Pain

Other?　　☐ ....　☐ ....

　　　　　☐ ....　☐ ....

Could this dream relate to a recent situation/event/person/problem in your life?

....

....

....

What is your interpretation of the dream?

....

....

....

....

....

....

....

In what way(s) does this dream affect you?
Does it provide clarity into something or suggest a specific course of action?

....

....

....

Made in the USA
Columbia, SC
09 December 2022

73062961R00070